Glass-eyed Paint
in the Rain

Other works by Laurie Wagner Buyer:

Blue Heron (Dry Crik Press)
Braintanning Buckskin (Dry Crik Press)

Glass-eyed Paint in the Rain

Laurie Wagner Buyer

HIGH PLAINS PRESS

FIRST PRINTING

1   3   5   7   9   8   6   4   2

Some of the poems in this book first appeared in other publications, some-times in earlier versions. Our thanks to the following publications: *College Poetry Review, Dry Crik Review, The Eagle's Cry, The Exponent, Fence Post, George Williams Review, Vietnam Generation, Western Pocket, Wish Women, Woman Spirit.*

Some poems were previously published in a chapbook by the author, *Blue Heron* (Dry Crik Press, 1995) and in the anthologies: *Maverick Western Verse* (Gibbs-Smith, 1994), *Cowboy Love Poetry: Verse From the Heart of the West* (Angel City Press, 1994), *The Cowgirl Companion* (Hyperion, 1993), *Graining the Mare* (Gibbs Smith, 1994), *The Anthology of Country Poetry* (1981), *Wordweavers* (Wyoming Writers, 1983), and *Wyoming Writing* (Wyoming Writers, 1980).

Library of Congress cataloging in publication data

Buyer, Laurie Wagner
Glass-eyed paint in the rain / Laurie Wagner Buyer.
p.   cm. -- (Poetry of the American West)
ISBN 0-931271-40-1 (alk. paper)
1. West (U.S.)--Poetry   I. Title.   II. Series.
PS3552.U8944G53   1996   96-32611
811'.54--dc20   CIP

HIGH PLAINS PRESS
539 CASSA ROAD
GLENDO, WY 82213
CATALOG AVAILABLE

For WFA
whose letters brought me West

and

For Mick
whose steadfastness gave me reason to stay

Contents

Rain Rhythm

Gathering Mint

E WOKE QUIET, ate potatoes and eggs
sitting alone on a cottonwood stump in the sun.

At noon he took a rifle, burlap bag, and handful
     of dried apples,
saddled the glass-eyed gelding, corraled
     the wayward mare,
whistled one long high note for the hound
     and was gone.

It was late the first summer, river running
     low, meadow grass tassels paled by wind.
I weeded the garden one faded row at a time
     while the goats lazed in barn shade
and the mare paced,
     nickering again and again.

He returned at dusk, drunk on solitude, singing
     in time with the gelding's rocky trot,
moccasined feet wet with mud,
     the burlap bag he tossed me
stuffed full of mint
     from the beaver slough.

A Good Woman

GOOD WOMAN sticks,
solid, unswerving,
molds herself to her man,
cooks and cleans and sews,
grows a garden to save on groceries,
rides whenever she can and
tries to rope, nurses calves,
fusses with chickens and rabbits
and children; she births and bathes and
beds, believing that somehow
her love can hold it all
together.

She cries alone, aching,
out behind the barn
or in the bathroom, water
running. Her smile lightens
every load but her own.
Her worn red hands grip and save,
surrender all she has to others.

A good woman sticks,
bends, gives, grieves in silence
until she comes
apart.

To Kill a Cat

SCRAWNY PIECE of life
you should have died at birth,
but I pushed the others away
and let you suck, gray
and white runt, all bones and fur.

He warned me, said you'd
never be strong, but I fed
you scraps on the sly, and opened
the window at night to feel you curl
by my side, share the fragile warmth.

Shaggy coats and snarls, your
brothers grew wild, hunted mice,
hissed and spat at a touch,
fought battles and finally
drove you away.

I cursed, threw rocks
at the culprits, searched
day after day in the pine woods
and cattail slough; "I told you,"
was what he said.

Weeks later, at dusk,
I rode the mare hell-bent for home;
you scurried cross the path—
dragging a crippled leg, starved,
eyes glazed—to crouch under red willow scrub.

I carried you to the cabin
in the crook of my arm,
fed you goat's milk from an eyedropper,
heard him say, not without pain,
you'd have to be put away.

My cat, my responsibility:
take it and kill it. I tried,
held you purring in my lap, the
morning sun warm on gray fur,
the ax handle poised in my hand.

Too hard to stun and strangle
his way, the master trapper's way,
so I stuffed you in a bag with rocks,
tied it tight with twine and
thought the river would be easy death.

But hearing the water roar
below the bank, you clawed
and screamed, till I let you out,
crying not for you, but for me,
too weak to do what must be done.

He must have watched from the window,
for he came then, without ceremony,
rifle in hand, and shot you sitting
there, green eyes blinking in the sun,
one shot behind the ear, that was all.

We buried you on the riverbank
beneath the aspens' quivering leaves,
and I loved him most because he dug
the shallow grave, laid you bleeding
to rest, held me close while I cried.

Scavenger

WE WALKED to Pack River that day
carrying tomahawk and fire-charred pot.

And you found, only two miles from camp, a dump
of rusted motors, broken bedsprings, and three
dozen dead calves sprawled bloating together.

Ignoring the stench, you squirmed between the bodies
and tomahawk swinging, cleaved each tiny head in two.

I scooped mottled tissue from skull to pot,
and crinkling my nose, smiled, knowing
only brains tan buckskin.

Indian Paintbrush

ALL DAY I cuss the cockeyed forest fence, broken
   wires, posts leaned over near the ground.

Snow weight's cruel in a country where nothing
   escapes the crush of seven feet deep.

Mosquitoes, deer flies, horse flies, add to
   the strain of too hot sun and no breeze.

Sweat damp, my glove cramped hands fight the stretchers,
   cranking hard to get that last bit of slack,

when the wire snaps,
                    tips my world in anger,

until I see one blood red patch in the dull sage
   nodding in a wayward breath of wind

before the fixed fence stretching tight against
   rolling ridges, each new splice silvery
   with reflected sun, each insect wing
   mirroring the light of another world.

Growing Tomatoes

—for Mom

ow OFTEN lately I've looked in a mirror
and seen you with my eyes—
not twin face and features,
but heart: a look alike copy
of what you feel for life.

Once, as a girl, you found a run-away
race horse near Maywood Park,
bliss-filled you galloped up and down
the cinder streets until
the authorities came
and took your dream away.

Always a finder of motherless things
you raised orphaned rabbits
and gophers,
swam the leech-ridden Des Plaines
hopped freights that took you west
to pick tomatoes all day for a quarter.

During my childhood I never
saw a wild rabbit
swam a river or
ate vine ripe tomatoes.
I saw the world from suburbs and Air Force
bases; begged you every Christmas
for a horse.

Years grew between us.
I cultivated my own world apart.

Then, this summer, in the Bear Paw Mountains
    I grew tomatoes for the first time
    and rode all day in the wind
    helping the hands sort cattle.

Feeling firm red fruit,
    sun and shadow,
    smooth rocking chair lope of the horse
    I knew I'd found you,
    in the heart
    that binds us,
    found in myself a re-creation
    of your childhood dreams.

Mud Creek Beaver

 ITTLE WORKER I've walked a mile in these hot, floppy irrigation boots to undo what you spent all night doing.

At dawn the water is not on the fields as it should be.
Of course you're the culprit, creator of deep ponds.

I search for you upstream, but now that your work is
done, you've gone under, hidden away from the sun.

Sighing, I slide down the steep bank into black water.
All night you cut willows, dabbed mud, building this dam.

Intricate and entwined, hard to dismantle, I spend hours
pulling each stick carefully, reversing your pattern.

Once I saw you sitting upright in the grass, balanced
by your broad tail, cleaning your rusty, oil-slick fur.

I caught you listening, stopped by some strange sound,
a half-chewed willow branch between your artistic paws.

At dusk I return, see you swimming circles in rosy light,
the whacking slap of your flat tail a wondrous warning.

I raise my rifle slowly, so very cold and heavy,
so uncompromising in my trembling, hesitant hands.

Scratchin' Brandy

SLICKER THAN a peeled onion,
sorrel coat a blaze of liquid fire
before the setting summer sun
he never comes when I call
but stands and waits, his ears
flicked forward in anticipation
of an early evening treat.

He chews. I scratch behind
his ears, his insect savaged chest,
along an itchy neck where his mane
hangs in silken splendor.

Stretching skyward, he curls
his lip in pleasure, then
stands spraddle-legged, his
nose nuzzling my shoulder.

No other lover ever responded
with such loose lipped ecstasy.

Trip up Tumble Creek

A DRUG OUT winter and a wicked deep snow spring
took its toll, twisted your hardened heart,
but the trip up Tumble Creek transformed you
even though you sat a knot-headed half-Arab
who was handraised and spoiled by a city woman
in a small round corral outside of Jackson Hole.

You called him "beetle brains" and soundly
cussed his stumbled trot, but you always
could get somethin' out of nothin' and
tried to make the best of what you'd got:
"At least I can catch the stupid SOB
and he don't even know how to buck!"

The day couldn't have been finer:
a bright blue sky hung over us like
a blessing and the sun was spring-kissed,
warm as toast on our winter-weathered faces.
Buffalo Peaks lay humped up, dark and solid,
under a heavy mass of roiling thunderheads.

"Gonna get our ass wet yet," you laughed
and gigged your stumblebum with the old 'gas feeds'
that used to be your Dads. My sorrel kept pace
and the silt burdened spill of the creek roared,
cascading over ancient beaver dams, swirling into
willow protected pools where the trout swayed hidden.

We ate our saddlebag lunch squat sitting on a log,
trading bites of apple and ham on bread while
the ground tied horses grazed on reborn bunch grass.
We held hands, hugged and kissed like teenagers,
giggled at the horses who watched our unusual
antics with wide eyed, jaw grinding bemusement.

You smelled of wind and sun, tasted as ripe
as the rich, piney earthed hillside where we stood.
Heading home in a drizzly rain, ten miles of posting
trot, our hats dripped, slickers flapped, and damp
boots creaked in time to hollow hoofbeat sounds.
Bone soaked, we unsaddled with weak, soggy laughter.

We stayed, arm in arm, to watch the horses drop and roll,
burden their sweaty backs with gray mud, whinny,
rear, then race away like mustangs to join their herd.
The cabin was warm, thick with the scent of soup and
dawn baked bread. We ate, then slept, the rain
rhythm and roar of the creek thrumming in our heads.

Purple Tulips

—for Kathy and Roz

FTER A weekend of Shakespeare
and talk and friends, the renewal of
feminine joys long since left by the way,
traffic pours into Denver as I alone turn
west into the mountains, heading home.

Kenosha rises in still-life splendor:
dark pines meld into darker skies,
billowing thunderheads pierced by
sun streams and a fleeting, startling
streak of bluest summer blue.

Whatever did we talk of ten hours
straight while we laughed and ate,
women cuddled in conversation,
finding comfort and a sheltered kind
of peace while it thundered and rained.

Home to me is a man and a dog waiting
by the gate. The simplest welcome
draws me into his embrace. He'll never
know of Eudora Welty or Anais Nin yet I
find wonder in our companionable silences.

Playing hard to catch, my sorrel hunkers
stockstill deep in the willow bottom
never knowing that his blaze face betrays him;
he's savvy, canny, holds his breath when
I jerk tight the cinch slack, strap on spurs.

Acceptance is part of age. How relaxing
finally to be able to giggle like girls at
ourselves, our men, our lives, the unfathomable,
intangible marks that brand each of our days
and nights as decidedly different, especial.

Riding to cattle he talks of grass and
sky and water, weight gain and culls,
whether to cut the hay this year or leave
it stand, thigh high and heavy headed,
waving amber tassels in the August wind.

Director of Development. Vice Principal.
I cannot seem to imagine your lives beyond
the executive titles as I unsaddle and stomp,
easing the ache in my knees. Ranch wife is
life to me now despite my city beginnings.

We've each worked so long to be where we are:
centered, happy. Never lost now, occasionally
wandering, wondering how to follow the myriad
directions of the heart that lead us further
and further apart from what we thought we'd be.

Before first light the black-crowned night heron
cries and cries…it will be all right
if we just remember to turn left at the purple
tulips, look for the sun's shadow on the edge
of the road; it will always bring us home.

Gentians

EARTH INTENT, my eyes scan
searching for flint chips, an arrowhead.
A warning prickle at my nape
makes me stop, look, a coyote
squatting on the trail, yellow eyes,
so close, intent on me.

Not a muscle moves, no sound
except the echo of my own fast pulse,
until he rises slowly, hobbles
four paces and stops to gaze again,
yellow eyes looking.

"Hello, Three Legs." I know
your story: how the neighbor's city
friend tried too long a shot, hit,
not quite a miss, enough frantic
fear and pain to last a lifetime.

Unafraid, you hobble, then wait,
curious of my two-legged stance,
a cast of dark long shadow ahead of low
gold-edged light. Hobble and stop.
Watch. Hobble and stop. Watch.

Sleek, vole fat, your fur is thick
grown already from the high mountains'
hard frost nights. No simple accident
this mysterious meeting,
this silent exchange of secrets.

No words come as I try to pray.
So I vow: when winter wearies you,
struggling and starved in the snow,
this time, I promise,
the rifle that's raised will be true.

Still, sheltered by a river willow's
gold-green leaves, you stay and watch.

I walk on, gathering fringed gentians
for a lone rock-marked grave.

Making the Bed

EVERY SUNDAY BEFORE first light
I strip the bed
roll up our worries
troubles, restless dreams
in the wrinkled sheets,
stuff them on top
the overloaded laundry basket.

I straighten the mattress
    where you've lain
    long and lean
    nearly every night
    of your adult life;
    where your children
    were conceived and carried;
    where your first wife
    left you curled and alone
    sleepless for so long.

It's an old bed burdened
    with pleasure and pain.

So I snap out fresh sheets
    whispered with wind
    sparkled with sun and sky
    smooth creases
    tuck corners tightly
    heave on the Hudson Bay blanket
    blue as your eyes
    black bordered and warm—
    the only thing I brought
    to our marriage bed
    except love.

Our second-hand spread
    is faded, raggedy edged, worn
    but it caresses us
    lets us sprawl across
    breathlessly
    boots and all.

Always I plump the pillows
    place them just so
    on this precious place
    where we lay and love
    forgive and forget
    each Sunday dawn
    starting clean and fresh.

Scarves

—for Catherine F. Atkinson

IN IRELAND
fifteen years ago
oceans away
from my mountain home
you bought me
two finely woven
woolen scarves—
orange and yellow,
blue and green,
to protect my fine hair
from the drying sun
and my delicate ears
from the cold winds
that came cascading
out of Canada
carrying loss and change.

I've worn one
or the other
of those soft scarves
nearly every day:
hiking dusk trails
picking wildflowers
weeding my garden
packing spring water
splitting stove wood
gathering cattle
feeding calves
checking heavy heifers
riding horseback
baling summer hay
skiing for winter mail
scouting for arrowheads.

You are old now,
over eighty and
edging away from me.
More than mother
more even than friend;
together we sheltered
secrets that even
sisters couldn't share.
Someday I will face
a lesser world
without you.
The scarves will keep
me safe, secure,
tying me
to hidden strengths
the close knit weave
we wove ourselves,
woman to woman.

Empty the High Country

When I Came West

WHEN I came west
I had never seen an elk, autumn dun
and bright buff, or heard an errant
owl ghost call from the thick shadow
of a pine, smelled the sharp tang
of wood smoke wreathed in my hair
or washed half naked in the glacial
spill rush of a river half a world away.

I never knew the gut deep intimate
warmth of milking goats, scattering
wheat for squabbling hens, the uncommon
joy of breaking bales for frost-crusted
horses, the mystery of unraveling a tale
of tracks and blood in the snow,
the silk-sand tongue of a cat washing
my stub-nailed and milk-stained hands.

In the remote rootcellar's dank
darkness, fear crawled over my skin,
dim candle light flickering over
thousands of hibernating daddy-longlegs
that clutched the ceiling in spidered clusters
as I knelt to rub away sandy soil from
strange roots—rutabaga, turnip, beet—
scrubbed them one by one on the riverbank.

Obscure spring soil gave up her bounty
of earthworms shoveled from their subterranean
sleep. Kissed by the newly awakened power
of the sun, I watched them writhe and weave
back into black earth where I planted
rows of peas and beans, coaxed strawberries
out of winter's wrap of mulch and straw,
rinsed my hands in a snow melt pond.

Loneliness lurked in my heart's smallest
corner. Once an enemy kept carefully
at bay by city lights I called her out face
to face everyday, tasted her name on my
silent tongue, turned her into an uncanny
comfort, wrapped her around me like fur,
danced with the dog, sang under the stars,
rode wild on a glass-eyed paint in the rain.

Coming Home

ORSES HOCK-deep in snow, miles
steaming from slick hides, bareback
on the appy, he pulls
the saddled paint behind.

The road ends here, where
mail stops, where plows
turn back for town, where
I wait in the mid-day quiet.

Loneliness ends here, beyond
the constant touch of other lives,
the beginning of the world,
lodgepole, willow and the river.

I am grateful the horses come, ears
perked in curious greeting, grateful
only his eyes speak, snow mingled in
graying hair he reaches out, packs me
close to the damp warmth,
takes me home.

Aspens after a Rain

SPENS AFTER a rain bend frost-glazed;
nights in October stretch out with cold.

A calf elk, lost from the herd, grazes
at last light with horses on mown fields

and cattle follow fence lines south
searching for open gates to better feed.

Storms empty the high country, leaving but
a few wintering with just wood for warmth.

I give you back your white world of
ghostly tracks and perfect silence.

Give me back the girl who once loved,
the crystal human sound of echoed laughter.

Hawk Watcher

OCTOBER MORNING, frost crisp
with a clarity that sent
farm voices reaching across distances
too great for eyes, a woman calling
children, a man whistling at his work.

We walked through fall fields
building up our height with inches
of dull clay mud that sucked and
stuck with every step. Your hawk
turned his hooded head atop your fist.

Out of breath I stopped to watch
a vision unfold across the oat hay
stubble—you, tireless, stretched
out in a run, the freed hawk circling
the sky in wait for a partridge

the pointing setter said was there.
Nothing flushed when you rushed the clump
of gold leafed brambles and the stiff
tailed dog trembled, sniffing here,
there for the invisible prey.

Looking aloft you feared the loss of him
too fond of flight to return without
reward. So from a leathern pouch at your
side you released a dove, her tiny eyes
taped shut so she could not see, yet, even so

her wings found the air and the freedom she
thought was there. She never saw the dark
shape twist and turn, never heard the sharp
report of impact at the bottom of the stoop
that sounded certain death: her clumsy

fluttering to the ground. We watched
the raptor land and stride to gain his prize.
Life feeds on life: his razor edged beak tore
her flesh, tossed dusk gray feathers to a
breeze that lifted and carried them away.

Enclosed in arms as strong and soft as wings,
I cannot sleep—the wide-winged hawk climbs
high on the windstream, the blind-eyed dove
beats beats her fragile, frantic wings.

Smell of Sage

AUTUMNS AGO we rode bareback for sage,
crossing and re-crossing river channels,
urging our mounts through ancient sloughs,
brush-choked islands. We talked then,
sometimes sang, passing the miles with
laughter until reaching the vista:

Sage creek poured out of Canada,
long bars of pebbled sand, and above,
a bluff so high we craned our necks
to see a wizened pine on top. The horses
tugged their bits, wanting to run;
we whooped and shouted, plunged cross
the creek mouth and down smooth bars;
sun and spray dazzling our eyes until
the horses lost all footing and swam,
wide-eyed and snorting for the bank.

The lone pine wore our dripping clothes,
your buckskins and moccasins, my socks and jeans—
the clash of cultures hanging in a tree—still,
stringing us together, our vision of mated
redtails circling the sky and the drifting
smell of sage.

Toweled by wind, we descended, the horses
haunch-sliding their way down rocky deer
trails. The flat was endless; a prehistoric
riverbed, aspen ringed, where now sagebrush grew.
Leaving the horses to trail their reins, we knelt,
snipped silver-green leaves into a leather pouch,
the herb to spice our sausage and stew, the pungent
odor filling our afternoon.

This autumn, returning to your world, I thought
that time lost to us. But, mid-winter, unknowing,
a visiting friend brought with her a sprig of sage.
By lamplight, watching you stitch a deer skin, she
unbraided and brushed my tangled hair. The smell
of sage reached us, seeping through our differences,
tying a loose, but lasting, common bond.

Loose Horse

L OOSE HORSE
on the horizon
the old cowboy
whirls away from
the herd, gallops
hard across gullies
up sage choked ridges,
finds the gelding down,
all froth and foam,
hind hoof through the
stirrup of a belly
turned saddle.

He walks slowly,
talks a murmur,
cuts the cinch,
gingerly jerks loose
the bleeding leg,
pulls the battered
grand prize saddle
aside while the horse
flails, struggles to
stand, stifled and
heaving in the bright
noon day sun.

He rolls a smoke,
hunkers down on his heels,
squints under the brim
of a black sweat-
stained hat and waits,
his dun ground tied
by his side. The bay
gelding quivers, head
low, rooted to the
earth by pain, the
chilling aftermath
of frenzied fear.

She walks slowly,
exhausted, bruised,
cradling an arm,
her injured pride,
her heavy heart,
remembering only
the sullen steer that
broke from the bridge
and raced for the ridge
as her barrel horse
cut back, the saddle
slipping, her body gone

rolling into the rocks
choking dust in her eyes
and all she could think
was "thank God I fell
free," as she lay
breathless watching her
panicked prize race away
into the gray-green land,
until the ridges rose
and he was gone from
view, with only the dim
direction of dust to follow.

"Well," he says, disgust
heavy in his nasal drawl,
"hurt?" She shakes her
head "no," buries her face
in her horse's thick mane
so he won't see her tears,
her fear, her aching
certain knowledge that
at seven her sleek
and sassy thoroughbred
will never run a
barrel or race again.

"Lead him slow," he orders.
"He's done; rub him down.
Come back for your gear…
and take those god-
damned roping reins
and burn 'em!" He swings
easily into his saddle
and trots effortlessly away,
after the scattered herd,
the day's long work
still to be done and
leaves her trembling, alone.

Anger burns in her dry
throat, bitter, sharp
as a knife and she spits
twice, raises her head,
her tumbled hair dirt
tangled and untamed.
She walks into the wind,
leading the limping bay,
never knowing that at night
in his frantic damning dreams
all he sees is a dark horse
loose on the horizon.

The Magpie

Snow came as I slept. Snow
once called "Ghost Face," long ago
before concrete and cars, when deer
in broken draws were more than moving
rifle targets and magpies in winter camp
were the sacred sign of plentiful times.

Walking downtown at dawn,
sidewalk trail already blazed
by newspaper boys and prowling cats,
the magpie squawked from a leaf-poor tree,
and the husky lay curled nose to tail
beside a discarded three-point deer head.

For blocks I watched the intruder flutter,
black and white, to the snowy lawn; alert
guard, with growled threats and lunges,
sent the hopeful scavenger back to perch
and stare, while he turned finical
circles and lay back down.

Coming home, the magpie still hopped patterns
in the snow, the husky watched by the ragged
head. I paused, let the wary sentry sniff
my hand, ripped off a chunk of fleshy hide,
left it as a simple offering
in the crooked branch of the willow tree.

This Place

—for Kathy and Joe

WE'RE NEWCOMERS, the deer old-
timers, more theirs than ours
the pond water they pause to drink,
the land they lie on near the house
that first night we called this place home.

Revelation comes mysteriously, on
nearly silent hooves, generations
of arced tracks mark the snow-quilted
earth as already taken, migration
routes far older than platted lots and
roads, a sacred deed though never written.

The deer that come to drink stop,
curious, all eyes and ears, watch
us watch them, flip their aristocratic
black tipped tails, spring away, reminding
us to tread lightly on this their treasured place.

Into Another Winter

HAY DOESN'T come the way it used to,
bale by bale out the back of a baler,
while the sun stretched out the days,
hot and dry, and circling hawks cast
black shadows along windrows and stubble
on our long loved and lost O Bar Y —

or like when you were a boy, singular
and shy, raking mown fields with horses
and the summer storms boiled out of rain-
maker's draw, making you unhitch and hurry
home, the team thundering behind while
lightning cracked close and balls of fire
raced along hail specked ground; your
mother on the far off white house porch,
apron whipping in the August wind,
shouting as if you could hear above
the wild roar, "Run, Mickey, Run!"

Now hay comes for the cattle on
semis, delivered in bulky square bales
that you move slowly and stack with
a backhoe, while I set the beastly
chain, mother up bale to bucket in a
haze of diesel smoke and dense fumes.

Changing, rearranging, the history
of hay marks the way we live our lives,
hanging still to a tattered remnant
of a dream, as the stacks reach high
against an October sky and the cows
come across the hand-built bridge,
trailing their calves into the warm
sun, the chill wind, the lesser light
that leads us into another winter.

Windstorms

RAIN PUFFS the dust summer gathered on the windowsill. Red-wing blackbird holds life closely on a wind tossed pine bough.

I've learned to lean into storms. Boughs are always
breaking, warmth and shelter are not easy to find.

Cold gusts whip away withered leaves. They test,
strengthen, leave bare ground for new growth.

My walls cannot weather steady buffeting; so I open
and close doors carefully, letting the gales pass through.

Pleasure and pain are variant velocities
of the same wind. Both make me bend.

Past Prime

AFTER A second snow
waving in steadfast wind,
their long stems bent,
bowed down gold and
gracious, I cut dried
grasses long past their prime.

I gather them in groups,
long and short, too different
to be dumped for compost,
too special to leave behind
destined for nothing but burial
in the long cold to come.

One by one, arranged in a
woven basket, their crescent
heads droop delicately, heavy
with spiked seeds, the memory
of sun and summer caught
in their flaxen sheen.

Geese

HOPPED ICE melts on the stove, to wash, then wring, then hang the clothes that stiffen like disjointed scarecrow limbs.

I eat fried slices from a deer's heart and watch
long icicles mirror leaden light through the window.

Shoveling, I search for drift hidden wood and hear
high on the numbing wind a single honk farewell

from an undulating ribbon
southbound in the sinking sky.

Marking Trail

CCUSTOMED TO black timber
I always sought shadowed spaces
long untouched by light
barely moved by wind.

Silence sustained me.

Cut deep, blazes there are old scars,
overgrown, sap-dried, secure.
Unseen, the trail is tangible
to foot touch, well-worn
under inches of pine duff
and scattered, decaying cones.

Now I've come to stand uncertain
on a sage-bristled hogback—
the path widens, fades, disappears,
lost in sunlit parks, seductive
with waving grass, windsong,
and far, far vistas, unblazed

unless I mark the way myself,
chip carefully, peel slowly
so the wounds won't ooze,
threaten to weep
and run like tears.

Caught in Silence

Under the Eclipse

 STRETCHED OUT rabbit shadows
wander atop the snow's bright crust,
eerie as unaccepted evening
under the eclipsed moon.

Before waking to walk,
I rolled in restless dreams,
your lost life regiven, granting me
one last grasping chance to hold you.

Aching emptiness enfolds me;
loss, like a lone rider, sings
just to hear a voice echo off a ridge,
spill across an open edge of sky.

I have never waited so long and hard
as I did on that night,
sitting on a frozen stump, waiting
for solemn stars to arc and fall.

Taste of Honey

STILL WINTER in my world,
I opened the box like Pandora
with quick childlike curiosity
and found the honey hidden there,
pale amber, rich as a jewel.

I could not wait for tea or bread
so I swirled it on my finger
and that first tentative taste
of sweetness on my tongue

was full of summer sun
and the fragile smell of flowers,
the harmonious hum of bees—
even the gentle feel of his hands
handling the swarming hives.

Madge

T HEY SAY SHE whacked off her hair
and crammed on a hat,
dressed like a man,
cussed and chewed,
married her hired hands
so she wouldn't have to
pay 'em any wages,
told 'em if they wanted
smokes and booze
to get off their butts
and trap for cash.

When they left, fed up,
she just married another,
outliving them all
until she dropped dead
of a heart attack
in front of the old wood range
while building biscuits.

Forty years later
I still felt her essence
coming down the stairs
into the cold kitchen;
I 'd light the lamp quickly
and save the single match
to fire up paper and kindling
carefully set in the stove.

"Move over, Madge," I'd whisper,
"Gonna have pancakes today."

At night her old homestead
house creaked and groaned,
keeping company with the wild
roar of the wide glacial river.
Every spring her crocus
and narcissus bloomed bright
below the south-face windows.

So far from town, no one
close enough to call or visit,
I found myself talking
to her when I was alone:

"Keep the fire goin' Madge,
I'm gonna shovel snow."

Skiing into the Storm

ATE MARCH snows lie waist deep, hard and crusted.
The first day of spring, I think, was last week.

Hollow moose feed on willow stubs thick as a thumb
and stand high on hind legs reaching for bitter pine tips.

Orphaned elk calves, saved by cut aspen branches,
lost in the end to a lion who spared only the leg bones.

Caught in a silence only I hear, I cook and clean and sew
and stare out at scudding clouds and new made drifts.

Snow pellets, blown by a west wind, glow in hazy light;
air like ice meets me as I leave, skiing into the storm.

Mick and the O Bar Y

THE RANCH lives in his eyes,
in storm gathered gray watching a thousand calves die,
in deep pools of blue mirroring the June smile of
grass greening up beneath retreating snow.

The ranch lives in his face,
still shadowed by a Stetson, shielding the wind-
carved furrows and sun-scarred skin, weathered
marks of tractor bound days getting the hay in.

The ranch lives in his hands,
gloved as ever, arthritis gnarled knuckles,
fingers curved forever from holding the lines
on 2-up, 4-up teams plunging through deep drifts.

The ranch lives in his arms,
sinewy still with bone grating shoulders
that pitched and shoveled and stacked, bucked
bales, carried kids and froze up calves.

The ranch lives in his knees,
barely hung together with chewed-up cartilage,
burning with too many years horseback, too many
miles kneeling, stretching up broken bottom wires.

The ranch lives in his feet,
shod in boots and overshoes and never nothin' else,
that walked or rode every square inch of sage,
timber, grass, never knew the meaning of rest.

The ranch lives in his heart,
parted now from those years of stinging sweat,
the "god-damned this" and "son-of-a-bitch that,"
everyday endearments of a man who loved his land.

Through Aspens and Beyond

UR WOODSTOVE blazes against winter.
Still the cold seeps in with silence.

Circling with wary snarls, this vicious
war worries us, frays us apart.

Years and years of sparring, skirmishes,
testing your strength against my weakness,

your right against my wrong—they say
knowing the enemy is half the battle—

but after all this precious time I know
nothing of your head, your heart, your cause;

I've only memorized the lean line of
your groin, the tight set of your jaw.

Our paths diverge. You forge through
pines to fight darkness encroaching;

I bend toward the light,
through aspens and beyond.

So It Snowed

 SOMETIMES HE'D come just to sit and look
through the waves of wind and snow
with only the old dog panting in his ear.

Everyone gone, south to town,
where winter was just a nuisance
to put up with until spring.

So it snowed; and he'd climb into
a giant tracked cat and crawl across
buried meadows to the grave marked point

where the ice-bound river bent around
twin banks and willow tops rose dappled
brown against white and blue shadowed acres.

Alone, looking south, he must have thought
how strange a world with his family gone,
how strange with only the hungry cattle,
the dog, the ancient, soothing quiet

and a forgotten generation's crumbling bones
beneath deepening drifts of benevolent snow.

The Gift of Water

ID-WINTER:
up to my chin in fragrant suds
my thighs red from the hot, hot water,
my sighs slipping out like an old mermaid's song
while I welcome your great gift:
an ancient chipped tub and no ration on water.

For I have washed clothes by hand,
water heated on a wood stove, hissing and steaming,
packed in heavy buckets from the ice choked river,
the sheets and shirts rinsed and wrung, hung in bitter
winds that chapped my cracked hands, leaving them
mapped with red lines and blue bulging veins.

And I have washed dishes by backcountry campfires
all black char and ash and earth, the precious water
carted carefully cup by cup from a hidden stone
gurgled spring and measured just so, leaving enough
for brushing teeth in pine patterned moonglow
and for morning's steeped and heady Earl Grey tea.

And I once washed myself standing in November snow,
five gallons from Tepee Creek stove heated and spared
for scrubbing my long length of unbraided hair,
the west wind iced tight my pale white skin
and pitcher dumped water brought forth drenched cries
that echoed through dark, still, star-rinsed skies.

Mid-winter:
no other gift has ever meant so much
as your abundance of well water,
pump primed, gas heated, tap delivered,
or the clean scoured warmth of my rosy skin
towel dried by your rough, ranch-worn hands.

Pitchfork: 15 Below

M Y HUSBAND's hands are curved
when he caresses me,
his fingers curled and cracked
with age and old arthritis.
Bucked bales and irrigation
shovels live there, along
with 4-up lines and latigos,
the sharp slope of my hip,
the worn softness of my sighs.

In December he leans
into a bitter, hard-bitten wind
and sleeve scrapes frost
from the hardwood handle
he holds like a long-time lover.
Sullen winter has him huddled
up into himself, tight and silent,
yet his far seeking eyes
see spring beneath pitched hay
and new fallen snow—

something I suddenly know, hard and
sure, that his hallowed hands
will never see again.

Healing

SOMETIMES I climb up
into the loft to sit,
surround myself in leather,
in the softness
of an antique chair
where I can look
a long way
across sage and grass
to the dark pines and
a white bright sky above the ridge.

The sun squats
above the wintered ridge
pierces through window glass
and grazes my face
gaining strength until
I am blanketed in rays
of warmth and the white
light that is the sky
fills an aching emptiness
that is my stony silence.

I sit in the half
darkness of near night
listening carefully
to a west wind that rises
out of the end of the day
and I hear answers,
long lost voices caught up
in the call of coyotes,
knowing I no longer remember
the questions never asked.

I let the light
come again out of the night
and I watch the dark
pines recreate themselves
along the high ridge and
the sage crawls out of the earth
to sit stoic and everlasting among
ancient grasses, lichened rocks,
and the horses come to stand, one by
one, in even ranks, soaking up the sun.

Elk in the Aspen

—for Melody

JUST OUT for exercise, the horses flip
crescent shaped snow clods from jogging
hooves. Haltered on a lead, the buckskin's
a brat, nipping my sorrel every other pace
until with canted eye I catch him in the act,
pop his velvet muzzle with the rope's end.

Overcast, damp, a chill breeze blunders
off cloud decked peaks in the west. A
mile past, on the river flat, I'd seen
elk trailing up this ridge... now I
watch, searching ranks of pale trunked
aspen, glancing for snow patched tracks.

Prick-eared, the horses scent them first,
flare their nostrils, fuss, shy sideways,
trot on under firm rein as I gaze and gaze
and finally see three cows, three calves,
perfectly camouflaged except for buff
colored butts and dark, coffee-cast manes.

Imagine the stretched wire gone, the graded
road grown over with grass, remember what
was can still be...horseback, a January
day, griseous and gray, just a glimpse
of elk in the aspen becomes a blessing,
a manifest reason to hold fast, to stay.

Cold in Sunshine

Eight Rabbits

 IGHT RABBITS hang skinned in pale spring sun. Old
dog gnaws patiently the severed heads, velvet ears.

In autumn I found his scrawled note, the rifle
missing. I was alone when the bloodhounds came.

Men swarmed through the woods, the hounds bayed low,
unsure. You rode through the dark hours searching.

By the corral, the orphaned colt sucking my fingers, I
knew the outcome. Bloodhounds won't go near a dead man.

Nothing to say, the silent months fade past. Still you watch,
questioning everything, even my rabbits, cold in the sunshine.

Song of Snowshoes

THE SONG OF showshoes was new to me that year, new as the oboe-song of the north wind, the measured voice of the ax chanting in the morning, the alto river humming beneath the ice.

Born in the city, I'd known no songs, no voice
sang to me at night, comfort for the growing fears;
at twenty I'd grown old on siren-wailed lullabies
and the traffic's endless dirge.

The land, the silence frightened me that year his
letters brought me west; novice at the window, I
watched the falling hush of snow, told him quietly
with longing, "I hear no special song."

Near the fire, half-skinned lynx in hand, his gaze
stole past me, past the window, to the horses turned
tail to wind, mute trio nodding thanksgiving
over broken alfalfa bales.

The evening star rose once without his coming home;
I worried by the window, but long before I saw him,
coyote 'cross his shoulders like a lamb, I heard
the swish of snowshoes along the riverbank.

Out of the still March night, born of winter silence,
came the softest rustling, the song of snowshoes,
welcome sound of return, the first unforgettable
song I heard of the land.

The World Never Turned for Mothers

IAH, THE world never turned for mothers,
never set its pace to the rocking of a cradle.
What else could we expect
that late March day
but 36 below.

Miah, old lop-eared goat,
I find you down at dawn
too fraught with labor
to nuzzle me as you always do.

I scratch behind your cut-off horns
see your eyes half closed in pain
lashes fringed with crystalline frost.

"Yes," I whisper, "I know it's cold."

What else can I do
but bring you blankets and
hold your head while you moan,
your blowed-up belly
twisted with kids waiting to be born.

You were the first goat
I ever had, old and patient
you calmly chewed your cud
while I worried your bag
anxious to milk out every last drop.

How much you taught me
in so short a time:
That comfort means shelter and feed,
that we give what we have, no strings attached,
that beauty (you cow-hocked & crooked jaw) lies inside us.

And now, at 36 below,
you teach me, without complaint,
fortitude and strength.

As hours creep by I apologize:
they never taught mid-wifery in school,
never told me how to ease your pain,
help you struggle through this wretched birth.

Running 'tween barn and cabin
I warm my hands, bring
you raisins and water which
you snuffle but will not taste.

No one's here to help us ... we,
like so many through the ages,
suffer alone with birth.

We wait. You grind your teeth
and moan. Blood and mucus
freeze like icicles on your tail.

All day we work together:
You push. I pull. And,
one by one, your breech-
birth kids are born.

Poor Miah, too tired to raise
your head and lick. I clean
your babies for you, carry
them towel-wrapped to the kitchen.

Finally, at dusk, when you're
able to rise, we wobble to
the canning shed. I light
a fire in the stove and whisper:
"Miah, please don't die."

All night I feed wood to the fire,
coax milk into sucking mouths,
watch you barely breathing,
your belly caved-in
shrunken by the life it lost.

Miah, the world never turned for mothers,
never set its pace to the hobbling of the old.
You never were the same after that torturous
birth. Often left behind, even your kids
followed the herd, while you stood cow-hocked
and alone in the sun.

That autumn, just after first snow,
you didn't come for evening milking.
I found you folded by a tree, your bag
shriveled and dry, too tired, too old
to even open your eyes.

The Way the Winter Was

HE WAY the winter was, the talking of sandhill cranes was music against still deep April snow.

Whooping, whooping their call echoed up the creek
where we worked the half-shepherd dog in harness.

I loved the sound as one never heard before;
you loved remembering all the years the pair nested here.

Nothing remained the same for us then, standing together
in clear spring light, watching sandhill cranes lift into flight.

Blue Heron

BLACKER THAN black slough earth
this hollow in your heart
deepened by loss and loneliness,
widened by countless wicked
winters, hard work and springs
that never gave a man a break.

Nothing but snow, wet, mud and muck,
sore-bagged, belligerent cows
and scour sick calves, finally
fodder for coyotes and ravens;
nothing but sick and tired of being
tired, bone weary and sinking,
sucked down deeper into the hole.

Every year it's worse, the worry
eats away our love like old rust,
weakening even the tensile tenderness,
the steel-hard, skin-soft bond of our
lovemaking, our sleepy holding tangle
of cramped legs and aching arms.

I have nothing left to give but this
great blue heron rising alone
from the river's open water,
winging its way into gray fog-
graced skies, leaving behind the snow-
skinned willows and ice-edged banks

the bawling, humped up cattle and my
freeze-dried tears falling like fire
into the last of the hay as I feed.

Winter Kill

 WIND BLOWS after the rain
from which direction
I cannot tell. I am lost again

except for raven cries
that call and I go

only to find a scattered remain—
fetid scraps, bones, bits of
hide and hair—

winter kill. I see no skull,
but here the tell-tale hoof:
a deer.

Ravens rise in mass
leaving me silence and the chance
to finger a chunk of tawny hair...

> *an old doe lays down*
> *at dusk on a snow bed*

> *alert, ears up, until the cold*
> *creeps in and freezes her liquid eyes*

I stretch out beside the cracked bones.

> *gold and graying hair*
> *twined tight in nests,*
> *bones rodent-gnawed to nubs*
> *'til nothing's left.*

Sighing,
the wet earth sucks at my warmth,
the ravens return, crying.

May Day

 HE YEARLING steer died the day after
the last calf of the season hit the ground.

Seven hundred bucks worth of coyote bait
and all the days of doctorin' gone sour.
"Kill 'em with kindness," you growled,
and were gone for the tractor to drag it,
stiff-legged and bloating, off to the gulch.

I watched from the steam curtained window
until the storm swallowed your bent back
and I was alone again with the dirty dishes,
stiff lipped with silence and unspoken blame.

I sat at my bill-piled desk, head in hands,
until I saw written on the feed store calendar
a bright promise penciled in last fall's hand:
May 1st—sow wildflowers.

Wrapped up well in worn boots,
tattered scarf, holey coat and gloves,
I stepped out into a swirl of stinging snow
to whirl and twirl, casting tiny seeds,
spinning like an insane sower
willing them with wordless prayers to grow.

Where the Cattle Walked

WHERE THE cattle walked
softened earth
raised crescent shaped
moons of mud,
iced by night
frozen into sharp peaks
that gouge my feet.

I see where the heifers slept
in the muck of the ranch road
so tired of snow and cold
they chose that miserly hint
of spring against their
thick, shaggy hides.

Stronger sun foreshadows
summer; their hair
irritates and itches
until they rub and scratch
stretch and yawn,
leave their winter robes
behind in torn tatters
snagged on barbed wire,
fence post nailheads
and broken willow branches.

Some tokens birds gather
for new nests,
others drift and blow,
rolling over and over
in the brisk west breeze.
A few stay stuck,
miniature decorations
left over from a holiday.

In the Mist

MIST HUGGED the riverbottom
on one of May's last mornings
when spring's green guise still seemed
an apparition following on the canvas
of winter's white hues.

I hiked breathlessly
wakened by the damp dawning,
until I came face to face with
an unearthly trinity of elk,
materializing majestically
out of the ethereal air.

Our vapor heavy breaths caught
collectively in a startled sigh,
suspended by surprise
while the roar of the river
echoed over the heart thud in my ears.

Then the spike sprang and jumped,
sent the top wire twanging
and the earth erupted into a furied
thunder of shod hooves, horses
and mules, streamed past in a liquid
gallop, trailing dewy manes and tails.

The cow and calf disappeared in a shroud
but I heard them hit the rushing water
and clatter up a rock bulged bank
while I watched and waited, trying to pierce
the whorls of white air, until at last
I saw them reborn on the ridge:
their buff butts wavered, adrift,
floating like the ghost-faced reflection
of a triune moon hung over rippled water.

A nebulous fogbow followed in their wake
and I found myself encircled by breathy,
velvet nostrils, sniffing and snorting
in curious disaffection, seeking to discover
if I was earthbound, ordinary, real.

Cookie's Colt

OOKIE'S COLT never had a chance,
no way close to full term, still
snuggled in its womb sack. You
scooped it up with the tined fork
and gave it delicately to the river's
icy, cleansing current.

Standing spraddled, head high,
defeated but still defiant,
Cookie arched her thick black tail
away from the blood and afterbirth
hanging angrily between her legs.

"She'll never do it again," you said
finally, haltered her tenderly and
led her away for her grain, doctoring
to be done, looking at long days
before acceptance settled in.

I stayed and stood alone on the barren
riverbank, aching for Cookie's emptiness,
twin to my own, aching for the slink
colt who'd never run a race against
the west wind and for you as I watched
a dream drift and die in your once
hopeful and believing blue eyes.

On the Upper Mikel's

CLUMPING ALONG a steep sidehill
laden with stretchers and splice wire
I stub my toe on broken shale,
skin my shin on a twisted stump
while sweat trickling beneath
my single cotton shirt
swears my boots shouldn't be soaked
by drifts of late tenacious snow.

I embrace the elements,
worship the new found sun and
walk my shadow deeper into day.

At noon I nurse numb hands,
dip naked feet in the frigid
spill of Rough and Tumble Creek.
A soggy sandwich and crushed
cookies taste unworldly,
fabulous as a feast.

Even your kiss, given shyly
under shelter of a shady pine,
comes graciously as a gift,
chides me tenderly
for hating to fix fence.

Serenade

T HE MOIST warm making
of another May
resurrects frogs from
their murky sleep,
fills the evening air
with impromptu serenades:
"Where love, where love," they sing.

I walk the slough edge
caressed by catkins
and absorb the sound
through every open pore,
wishing I could slip
this heavy human skin
and shed the knowing,
slide down into the mire
and join the calling chorus
in the enchanted grass,
my throat bulged with song,
one beauteous eye courting,
the other cocked and wary
of the wading, waiting heron.

In the Shadow of Black Mountain
—for Violet, 1926-1995

ON THE MORNING of the day she died
the redwing blackbirds returned,
singing as ever spring's song
liquid trills and rushes like water
   spilling free after winter's bondage.

On the day they lowered her
in the cold, hard ground
fog folded up the hills
and the snow returned
soft and silent as a prayer.

Rare and wonderful
delicate as a Rocky Mountain Lily
she lived her whole life
in the shadow of Black Mountain
and sheltered her fragile heart.

Happiness was the haven of home
and the run of the ranch
the feel of a fine horse
between her legs and a length
of worn leather rein in her hand.

She broke colts, drove teams,
cared for her cattle, herded sheep,
kept close to the old ways and
treasured the simplest of things:
a wood fire, flowers, wild birds.

On the day they lowered her
into the cold, dark ground
the pines wore lacy frozen frocks
as lovely as virgin brides
in the shadow of the mountain.

Willow Bender

OWED DOWN like river ballerinas
graceful and poised
shouldering unforeseen snow,
willows bend and breathe
the weather with such dignity
I cannot cuss or complain.

Instead I take blackbird notes
and make them into a mantra
which I whisper over and over again
as I shovel sodden haystacks,
the diminishing woodpile and walkways.

When the sun returns
I straighten my curved back and
stretch, dancing off my burden,
toss back a strand of silky hair
and blossom like a pussy willow.

LAURIE WAGNER BUYER was born in Scotland, raised in suburbs and on Air Force bases around the world, but found a home in the West.

She came West in 1975 with a backpack and twenty-five dollars in cash. She thought she would stay one winter and she ended up staying for life.

Since 1988 she and her husband Mick, a rancher, have lived on the South Platte River near Fairplay, Colorado, where they run a cow-calf operation. Previously she has lived on ranches in both Wyoming and Montana.

*The text is composed
in twelve-point Adobe Garamond.
Display is Tagliente, based on the copybooks
of a renowned sixteenth-century Italian writing master,
created by the Judith Sutcliffe, the Electronic Typographer.*

*The book is printed on
sixty-pound Glatfelter Supple Opaque,
an elemental chlorine-free,
acid-free recycled paper
by Thomson-Shore.*